D0913193

A BOOK OF ROSES

With sixteen colour plates after the originals in
REDOUTÉ'S "ROSES"
and text by

J. RAMSBOTTOM

The KING PENGUIN *Books*
PUBLISHED BY PENGUIN BOOKS LTD. HARMONDSWORTH
MIDDLESEX ENGLAND

The King Penguin Books : edited by Elizabeth Senior

THIS VOLUME PUBLISHED 1939

Made and printed in Great Britain by
ADPRINT LTD. AND HENDERSON & SPALDING LTD.

CONTENTS

" She wrayeth her thorn with fayr colour and good smell. Among all floures of the worlde the floure of the rose is cheyf and beeryth ye pryse. And by cause of vertues and sweete smelle and savour. For by fayrnesse they fede the syghte : and playseth the smelle by odour, the touche by softe handlynge. And wythstondeth and socouryth by vertue ayenst many syknesses and evylles." So we read in a translation of one of the earliest printed books, *Liber de proprietatibus rerum*, which was probably written about the middle of the thirteenth century. It was printed in 1472 and a translation by Trevisa was printed by Caxton's apprentice and successor Wynkyn de Worde in 1495.

No flower has been so popular in the past as the rose, and, in spite of the introduction of other plants from all parts of the world, it retains its pre-eminence. It is therefore easy to understand why it figures so largely in literature and art and plays its part even in history and religion. Many scientific treatises have been devoted to the description of the species and varieties of roses, several of them with illustrations. The most famous of them all is *Les Roses* by P. J. Redouté. The first edition of this magnificent work is in three folio volumes which were published in Paris (1817–1824) in thirty parts, each, as a rule, composed of three sheets of text and six plates ; the text was by C. A. Thory. Two other editions were published, one in forty parts (1824–1826), and the other in eight single and eleven double parts (1828–1830) ; both these are octavo, and the plates are much inferior to those of the folio edition.

Pierre-Joseph Redouté (1759–1840), " le Raphaël des

fleurs," was born at St. Hubert in the province of Liège. He was the grandson, son, and brother of artists. He learned the principles of art from his father, and before he was fifteen he left home to wander round Flanders and Holland studying the works of the native schools. He was inspired by the celebrated floral compositions of Van Huysum and Seeghers but, having to paint in order to live, he undertook the decoration of churches and castles, the traditional art of his family. After several years passed in this way he returned to St. Hubert and the reputation he had gained soon brought him commissions to paint portraits of the most prominent people of Luxembourg. But this did not satisfy him and he turned to Paris, characteristically losing the letters of introduction given him by a princess devoted to the arts. Fortunately he was able to join forces with his brother Antoine Ferdinand, who was engaged in decorative painting, and this gave him some scope for the kind of floral decoration which pleased rococo taste.

Some of his paintings of flowers came to the notice of G. van Spaendonck, the famous botanical artist, " peintre ordinaire du Roi pour la miniature," who employed him to do some of the paintings on vellum for the royal collection, teaching him the necessary details. This collection was begun by Gaston d'Orléans and, when he died in 1660, the paintings passed to Louis XIV and his artist, N. Robert, was engaged to carry on the work. Twenty paintings, chiefly of plants but some of animals, were added annually. At the Revolution the collection was transferred to the Jardin des Plantes and Spaendonck was appointed Professor of Iconography. Redouté succeeded him in 1822 but his title was " maître de dessin pour les plantes " ; the animal paintings were not in his charge. He introduced the method of working in water colour instead of the customary gouache, so gaining

PIERRE-JOSEPH REDOUTÉ (aet. 59)

transparency and preventing scaling. Additions were regularly made to the collection of vellums for many years after Redouté's death, but gradually less attention was given to them and the last painting was made in 1905.

The first botanist to recognise Redouté's skill was L'Héritier de Brutelle, who was at that time working at the Peruvian plants collected by Dombey. Shortly afterwards, owing to representations made by the Spanish government, L'Héritier was ordered to hand over these collections to Buffon, then Director of the Royal Botanic Garden. Instead, he brought them to London and, until the Revolution, worked at them in the library of Sir Joseph Banks. Redouté accompanied him in order to learn the English methods of stipple engraving, not then used in France. He illustrated several important botanical monographs, but his reputation rests mainly upon the works published in his own name. The first of these was *Les Liliacées* (1802–1816), in eight folio volumes with 486 coloured plates. It was dedicated to the Empress Josephine, whom he served as floral artist, and appeared under the auspices of the Minister of the Interior. This magnificent work, widely distributed to distinguished artists and foreign sovereigns, made Redouté famous, but the seal was set on his reputation by the prodigious success of his *Les Roses*, a success even more remarkable in that it has continued to the present time. Josephine was noted for her love of roses, which provided her chief consolation in her retirement at Malmaison where she aimed at growing all known forms. As a memento of her inspiration to rose-growing in France the rose garden at Malmaison has been reconstructed and planted with as many as possible of the roses known to her.

Redouté's official duties included the giving of lectures, and several of his women pupils gained fame. He also taught several royal ladies.

Having regard to his delicate portraits of plants, his long

8

tenure of government service through successive upheavals, his friendship with ladies of the royal family and his success as a teacher, we hardly expect to learn that he had the appearance of a working gardener and thick and deformed hands like a navvy's. In all he is said to have painted over a thousand roses.

*   *   *

Although in the authorized version of the Bible the word rose is twice mentioned, " I am the rose of Sharon " (*Cant.* 2, 1) and "The desert shall rejoice, and blossom as the rose" (*Isaiah* 35, 1), it is a translation of the Hebrew word *hăbaçéleth* which indicates a bulbous plant and may refer to the sweetly scented Narcissus (*N. Tazetta*) which grows in Palestine and is much appreciated by the natives.

When we turn to the Apocrypha, however, there are certain passages which seem undoubtedly to refer to the rose, but at the time of the Babylonian Captivity : thus " Let us crown ourselves with rose buds " (*Wisdom of Solomon* 2, 8). This reference to crowning with rose buds is interesting. It may be that the custom of wearing floral garlands was borrowed by the Greeks and Romans, but it is more likely that so obvious and attractive a method of personal adornment arose independently among different nations and had no common origin.

The rose was beloved of the Greeks and Romans. In the Odyssey there is the well-known figurative "rosy fingered dawn," and in the Iliad, Aphrodite prepares Hector's dead body with oil of roses. According to tradition, Sappho was loud in her praises of the rose and christened it the " Queen of Flowers." Other Greek poets praise it, among them Theocritus, Bion and Anacreon.

Herodotus, the Father of History, gives the first account of a double rose in the gardens of Midas, " in which wild roses grew, each one having sixty leaves, surpassing all

9

others in fragrance." It is generally agreed that this rose was the Cabbage Rose, *Rosa centifolia*.

From the Father of History we turn to the Father of Botany, Theophrastus, the pupil of Plato and Aristotle. His *Enquiry into Plants* contains the first botanical accounts of numerous plants, including the rose. "Among roses there are many differences, in the number of petals, in roughness, in beauty of colour, and in sweetness of scent. Most have five petals, but some have twelve or twenty, and some a great many more than these ; for there are some, they say, which are even called 'hundred-petalled.' Most of such roses grow near Philippi ; for the people of that place get them on Mount Pangaeus, where they are abundant, and plant them. However the inner petals are very small (the way in which they are produced being such that some are outside, some inside). Some kinds are not fragrant nor of large size. Among those which have large flowers those in which the part below the flower is rough are the more fragrant. In general, as has been said, good colour and scent depend upon locality ; for even bushes which are growing in the same soil shew some variation in the presence or absence of a sweet scent. Sweetest-scented of all are the roses of Cyrene, wherefore the perfume made from these is the sweetest. . . . Roses can be grown from seed, which is to be found below the flower in the 'apple'. . . . As however the plant comes slowly from seed, they make cuttings of the stem, as has been said, and plant them. If the bush is burnt or cut over, it bears better flowers ; for, if left to itself, it grows luxuriantly and makes too much wood. Also it has to be often transplanted ; for then, they say, the roses are improved." Other facts about roses can be gathered from his comparisons ; it appears that the roses he knew were either white or pink.

The earliest known European illustration of the rose is

in the House of Frescoes at Knossus, Crete, and dates from about the middle of the sixteenth century B.C. The flowers have six petals instead of five, and are golden rose colour with orange centres dotted with deep red. The leaves are also conventionalised. So far as is known the only representation of a rose dating from Grecian days is on the coins of Rhodes, where roses were of sufficient significance to give their name to the island. Roses are shown on coins at other places. Thus our Rose Noble of the fifteenth and sixteenth centuries was so-called because it had the figure of a rose stamped on it.

The Romans were no less lavish than the Greeks in their praise of the rose. Among poets Virgil, Ovid, Horace and Juvenal sing of its charms ; and Cicero and Columella write of them. Pliny in his *Natural History* mentions twelve varieties, naming them from the places where they grew. " The essential points of difference in the rose are the number of the petals, the comparative number of thorns on the stem, the colour, and the smell. The number of the petals, which is never less than five, goes on increasing in amount, till we find one variety with as many as a hundred, and thence known as the *centifolia.*"

Perhaps even more notable than their praise of the rose is the extravagant use the Romans made of it in their festivities for which they cultivated it on a considerable scale in various favourable districts. The prettiest girls sold them, their names were immortalised by the poets, and *mea rosa* was a term of endearment. Wreaths of roses crowned heads at banquets where unwise revelations, if made, were *sub rosa.* Flowers, and particularly roses, became more and more an obsession, tables, couches, streets and even lakes being strewn with them. Suetonius relates that Nero spent four million sesterces in procuring roses for a single feast.

The rose, the emblem of love, was given by Cupid as a bribe to Harpocrates, the god of Silence, whence originated the custom in northern countries of suspending a rose from the ceiling at meetings where secrecy was enjoined. Carvings of roses are seen on the ceilings of old dining-halls in this country and are probably the origin of the "ceiling rose," the ornamental centre-piece of the ceilings of most Victorian houses.

The ancient Egyptians did not know the rose. It does not figure on any monument at the time of the Pharaohs. It is only from the time of the Ptolemys (B.C. 308 onwards) that traces of the flower are found or represented on textiles and dried frescoes. Garlands of roses, rose buds and rose petals have been found in several Egyptian tombs dating from 100-300 A.D.; the species appears always to be *Rosa sancta*. In the tomb of the female magician Myrithis, dating from the third century, a quantity of petals and buds of *Rosa sancta* were found, also a silken mantle with a bright pink ground strewn with five-petalled yellow roses. "Colouring in Egypt has always been conventional, and the yellow particularly represented everything imported from the East, or even to specify from the country of 'Pount' (Arabia), meaning by that that the Arabian coast was the passage way for importations." The probability is that it was introduced by the Greeks. At the time of Cleopatra the rose had its part in all ceremonies as in Greece and Rome. Wreaths were made almost exclusively of roses which gradually entirely replaced the lotus.

It is not surprising that the Early Fathers of the Church looked with disfavour on the wearing of garlands and crowns so closely associated with Roman conviviality and even debauchery. The rose, as it figured most prominently, was especially disapproved of. Before long, however, it became the emblem for those who triumphed over persecution, and for martyrs. The Christian mystics developed its symbolic usage, and the five petals of the red rose typified the five wounds of Christ, the white rose the Virginity of the Blessed Virgin.

Flowers played an important part in the services of the Church in England during the Middle Ages, in crowning the priests, wreathing candles or adorning shrines. Gardens were made within the monastery walls for providing the flowers and they were under the charge of the Sacristan. There was a *gardina sacristae* at Winchester as early as the ninth century, and Henry VI bequeathed such a garden to the Church of Eton College. " At all great functions, both during the processions or while performing the services the priests were crowned with flowers. This was especially the custom at St. Paul's, in London, and when on June 30th, 1405, Bishop Roger de Walden was installed there, he and the Canons of the Cathedral walked in solemn procession, wearing garlands of red roses." The wearing of *coronae sacerdotales* lasted for several centuries to end only with the Reformation.

In addition to this use in religious ceremonies the rose often figures as an ecclesiastical emblem. Thus the Golden Rose of the Church of Rome, dating probably from the fourteenth century, is blessed by the Pope on Laetare— Rose Sunday—and is occasionally bestowed on any person or institution especially distinguished in the Catholic Faith. The flower is also associated with many Saints and particularly with the Virgin. It has its place, too, in church architecture in the Gothic rose windows. At York Minster, where there is a well-known example, an inscription on the door of the Chapter House suggests that the rose was regarded as an emblem of perfection : *Ut rosa phlos phlorum sic est domus ista domorum* (As the rose is the flower of flowers, so is this house the house of houses).

The rose also was sometimes used for rents. Part of the

rent paid by Elizabeth's Lord Chancellor, Sir Christopher Hatton, for Ely Place, was a red rose; the quit rent for the Star Hotel at Worcester was "one red rose delivered on 24th June of each year."

The rose plays a prominent part in English heraldry. True heraldry was introduced into this country in the second half of the twelfth century and during the reign of Henry III (1216–1272) became systematised, with its own technical language. When every person of prominence bore heraldic arms wide choice had to be made for suitable devices (charges), and the rose figures prominently among these. Four types are recognised : (1) The most usual is a five-petalled rose with a large seeded centre, and five short sharp-pointed leaf-like sepals projecting slightly between the petals; the parts may be emblazoned in any of the five heraldic colours, the term "seeded" being used if the centre, and "barbed" if the sepals are differently tinctured from the petals. (2) The Tudor Rose is always double, usually with a white inner and red outer row of petals, an heraldic device for uniting the emblems of York and Lancaster. There are beautiful examples in Henry VII's chapel, Westminster Abbey. (3) The Rose-en-Soleil is a white single or double rose displayed in the centre of a golden-rayed sun. In its single form it was first used by Edward IV after the Yorkist victory at Mortimer's Cross ; the double form appears on the Regimental Colours of the Fifth Company of the Grenadier Guards. (4) The Slipped Rose, a flower with remains of the stalk and attached leaves, when surmounted by an Imperial Crown, forms the Badge of England.

A Chaplet of Roses is composed either of four roses arranged at equal distances round a circle with intervening leaves or may consist entirely of roses. In days of chivalry it was granted to gallant knights for acts of courtesy.

Marks of cadency are used to distinguish the arms of a son from those of his father. A seventh son bears his father's arms with a small-scale rose in the chief centre point. Other forms of differentiating by means of the rose are used in Royal heraldry.

The rose has been a favourite badge with the Sovereigns of England. The badge of Edward I was a golden heraldic rose stalked proper; one of Henry IV was a red rose; that of Edward IV a white rose-en-soleil; Henry VII and Henry VIII used a Tudor rose crowned; Edward VI a Tudor rose impaling a pomegranate; Elizabeth a Tudor rose with the motto *Rosa sine spina* (a rose without a thorn); the Stuarts a thistle and a rose dimidiated (vertically halved and the two outer halves conjoined) and crowned, and Queen Anne a rose and thistle both growing from the same stem, as may be seen to-day in the King's Colour of the 2nd Battalion Scots Guards.

It is improbable that the rose became the emblem of England by being deliberately chosen as the most appropriate flower. The reason for its choice is apparently historical. About the year 1277 Edmund Langley, first Earl of Lancaster, second son of Henry III, who had acquired with his wife the County of Champagne, was sent by the King of France to Provins to avenge the murder of the mayor of the city, who had been assassinated in some tumult. He remained at Provins for a considerable period, and on his return to England took for his device the red rose of Provins. The Rose of Lancaster was probably the Damask Rose, though it may have been the French Rose which was also cultivated at Provins. Presumably, the Rose of York was chosen in distinction, though probably not in so dramatic a manner as Shakespeare relates in Henry VI.

*   *   *

The genus *Rosa* (that is the plants which we call roses)

has a wide distribution in the north temperate zone ; a few species occur on tropical mountains. It should not be overlooked that when writers speak of the introduction of roses to this country they are referring to the old garden forms. We have our British species which, though few, have a charm of their own. If it be asked, however, how many native British species there are the question is not easy to answer, for as in the allied genus *Rubus*, which includes the blackberry and raspberry, the species may be regarded as few and variable or many and constant according to the criteria of differentiation adopted. The most recent enumeration gives " about 16 species, 110 varieties and 48 forms, also 28 hybrids." The problems encountered here and in similar genera are amongst the most interesting that occupy the attention of modern investigators but they are too complicated to consider in a few words. For our present purpose we may regard our native species as *Rosa canina*, the Dog Rose ; *R. arvensis*, the Trailing Rose ; *R. eglanteria,* the Sweet Briar ; *R. spinosissima*, the Burnet or Scotch Rose ; *R. tomentosa* ; and *R. micrantha*. These species all have a very wide distribution in Europe.

Most species introduced to British gardens in recent years have been collected by botanical explorers. The seeds have generally been accompanied by herbarium specimens and there is usually little or no doubt about the date of their introduction or their native habitat. It is not so with many of the old garden roses. Frequently definite dates are given, but it is often overlooked that some may have been in cultivation here before the time of the herbalists. The ancient Briton apparently had little, if any, knowledge of horticulture, but the Romans during their three and a half centuries of colonisation built villas and lived as nearly as possible in their accustomed manner. They doubtless introduced plants from home for their gardens and probably roses were amongst them. With the

16

arrival of the Teutons most traces of culture were lost until the introduction of Christianity. There was a revival of interest in plants when monasteries were established with gardens attached to them for the growing of vegetables and herbs, not necessarily drab-looking plants, for roses and other brightly coloured flowers had their medicinal uses. The close connection of the monasteries with those of the Continent would certainly encourage the exchange of useful species, and possibly others would be introduced because of attractive associations. The Crusaders also are generally understood to have brought seeds and plants home from their campaigns in the manner characteristic of soldiers. Members of the Hanseatic League and the Staple of Calais in their trading brought plants from over-seas. We have at present only a meagre knowledge of the contents of any garden existing before the end of the sixteenth century. The earliest printed catalogue is that of Gerard's garden in Holborn, which is dated 1596. Sixteen roses are listed but with Latin names ; their English names are given with descriptions in *The Herball or Generall Historie of Plantes* of 1597 : The English white Rose single, the white Rose double, the red Rose, the great red Rose, or red Prouince Rose, the Great Holand Rose, commonly called the Prouince Rose, the common Damask Rose, the single Muske Rose, the double Muske Rose, Spanish Muske Rose, Veluet Rose, Yellow Rose, the Pimpernell Rose, the common Sweete brier, the double Sweete brier, the cinnamon Rose, and the double cinnamon Rose.

It is worth noting that the list includes British species, and further that some of these were special forms which had probably arisen in cultivation, possibly as " sports " or by crossing, though such forms might occur in the wild. Thus Gerard writes, " The double white Rose doth growe wilde in many hedges of Lancashire in great abundance, even as Briers do with us in these southerly parts." It was probably a natural sport of *Rosa arvensis*.

Roses were grown in some quantity not only for aesthetic reasons but also for their use in a number of preparations —melrosette, sugar roset, syrope of Rooses, oyle of roses, and rose water are mentioned in Banckes's Herbal (1550): " also drye roses put to ye nose to smell do cõforte the braine and the harte and quencheth sprite." Rose water was practically the only perfume for centuries, and it was also used for washing and purifying. It is interesting to trace the rapid rise of the knowledge of plants in relation to Elizabethan adventure. John Parkinson, whose garden was in Long Acre, says in his *Paradisi in Sole Paridisus Terrestris* (1629) that he had " to furnish this garden thirty sorts at the least, every one notably differing from the other, and all fit to be here entertained."

There are numerous emblematic and allegorical notices of the rose in Shakespeare's works suggesting that the knowledge of the kinds he mentioned was widespread.

Double roses have been in existence as far back as we have record. They are monstrous flowers in that many, or even all, of their stamens are metamorphosed into petals.

At the Renaissance great attention was paid to the classical writers, and the remarks of Theophrastus that though roses grew from seed they were more easily propagated by cuttings influenced gardeners. There was no great advance in rose production until roses were grown from seed, and Holland was first in this. Previously, new forms could be obtained only by selection or from sports. When seeds were sown new plants sometimes occurred through accidental crossing. Finally the stage was reached when artificial crossing was practised.

When seeds are sown from roses which have been cross-pollinated the resulting generation is not "fixed." With repeated crossing more and more uncertainty results.

The only way of continuing a given form is by reproducing it vegetatively. To do this cuttings are planted, or dwarf or bush roses may be layered, or if the rose forms suckers these can be separated. Grafting and budding are commonly practised, particularly the latter; Manetti (often used as stock) is an Italian rose raised in the Milan Botanical Garden about 1837. Modern garden roses differ greatly from those of a century ago in form, colour, length of flowering period and to some extent in fragrance. At the beginning of last century all roses were summer-flowering except the Chinese Monthly Rose, which flowered also in autumn.

Several main groups of roses have been in favour during the past century or so. The Bourbon Rose (x *Rosa borbonica*) is presumably a cross between the Chinese Monthly Rose and the French Rose, the only two forms then grown on the Île de Bourbon (Island of Reunion) off the east coast of Africa, where it arose spontaneously about 1817.

The Noisette Rose (x *Rosa Noisettiana*) was raised in America by J. Champney and introduced to Europe by P. Noisette : it is White Musk Rose crossed with Chinese Monthly Rose.

The Tea Rose dates from about 1830, when the " ever-blooming " Blush Sweet-scented Chinese Rose (which was introduced to this country in 1809) was crossed with Yellow Tea-scented Rose (introduced 1824).

The Hybrid Perpetual is the offspring of the Damask Rose, French Rose and the Hybrid China.

The Hybrid Tea is Hybrid Perpetual crossed with Tea Rose. This is now the most popular type in this country.

The Pernetiana type is the result of a cross between the Persian Yellow Rose (*Rosa lutea*, introduced in 1830) and Hybrid Tea, first made by Pernet-Doucher about 1900.

The Wichuraiana hybrids have been derived from *Rosa*

Wichuraiana, a Japanese species with evergreen foliage introduced to Europe in 1886. These modern Ramblers, of which the first and best known is Dorothy Perkins dating from 1902, originated from R. *Wichuraiana* crossed with Hybrid Perpetual.

So much mixing has gone on amongst the thousands of varieties that it is very difficult to decide to which of the many groups a new rose belongs.

However this may be, Gerard's words still hold : " the Rose doth deserve the chiefest and most principall place among all flowers whatsoever, being not onely esteemed for his beautie, vertues, and his flagrant and odoriferous smell ; but also bicause it is the honor and ornament of our English Scepter."

* * *

In the selection of sixteen plates of Redouté's *Les Roses* an attempt has been made to combine the artistic and the scientific. The descriptions follow the order of the reproductions. Where there is an English popular name that is given and is followed by the Latin name used in Miss Willmott's *The Genus Rosa* ; if the Latin name on Redouté's plate is different it is given in brackets.

DESCRIPTIONS OF PLATES

PLATE I

ROSA NITIDA (*Rosa Redutea* var. *rubescens*)

This species is native in the region between Newfoundland and eastern Massachusetts, occurring on the margins of swamps and low-lying places. It was first collected by Sir Joseph Banks on his expedition to Newfoundland in 1776 with D. Solander, and their dried specimen is in the British Museum Herbarium. The plant is dwarf in habit and has narrow glossy leaflets which redden in autumn, dense and very unequal red prickles, and bright red branches.

PLATE II

YELLOW AUSTRIAN BRIAR
ROSA FOETIDA (R. *Eglanteria*)

This species and its copper-coloured variety (*see* Plate IV) are included in Gerard's Catalogue but nothing is known of their introduction. Both occur wild from the Crimea to Tibet.

The small, rounded, sharply toothed, glaucous green leaflets and the shiny, glistening, chocolate-coloured stems are characteristic of the Yellow and Copper Austrian Briars and of the Persian Yellow. The flowers have a slightly fetid smell.

PLATE III

APPLE ROSE
ROSA POMIFERA (R. *villosa*)

This rose is widely distributed in central Europe and
though it occurs in Scandinavia it does not reach this
country. It has long been cultivated here chiefly for its
large handsome rich deep-red fruits. It crosses freely
with other species.

PLATE IV

COPPER AUSTRIAN BRIAR
ROSA FOETIDA var. BICOLOR
(R. *Eglanteria* var. *punicea*)

This appears to be a variety of the Yellow Austrian Rose
which is not quite fixed for it is not unusual to find pure
yellow and copper-coloured flowers on the same bush,
or flowers of two colours, or even bi-coloured petals.

PLATE V

DOG ROSE
ROSA CANINA [var. NITENS]

The Dog Rose is the common wild rose of our hedges.
Considered in a wide sense this species is distributed
throughout Europe and reaches north Africa and western
Asia. It includes a very large number of named forms.
The prefix " dog " is often depreciatory as in the scentless
dog-violet, but here it is a translation of the Latin name,
which was derived from the Greek *Cynorrhodon* used by
Theophrastus, who did not regard it as a true rose. It
has been suggested that the name might refer to the
plant having been used as a remedy for the bite of a

mad dog, or alternatively dogs may have been supposed to eat the hips.

The Dog Rose though probably always cultivated in this country has not influenced garden roses to any extent. The form illustrated has shiny leaves.

PLATE VI

ROSA MUNDI
ROSA GALLICA var. VERSICOLOR

Rosa gallica, the French or Garden Rose, has been found wild in various parts of Europe. Its dwarf upright and compact habit, absence of large thorns, and its dark thick leaves readily distinguish it. The species was much grown formerly for the preparation of conserve of roses and infusion of roses, which were long retained in medicine for their agreeable qualities rather than for any special value. It is the French Rose which is usually figured in stained glass windows.

Innumerable varieties have arisen in cultivation. The most striking of these is Rosa Mundi, of which there is a fine drawing by Robert, dated 1640, in the collection of vellums at the Jardin des Plantes. It is said to derive its quaint name from Fair Rosamund, the mistress of Henry II. The date of its introduction to this country is not known. (The York and Lancaster Rose is a variegated variety of the Damask Rose.)

PLATE VII

ROSA MICRANTHA var. ANEMONEFLORA
(R. *rubiginosa* var. *Anemoneflora*)

The present Rose is a garden variety with flowers like an *Anemone*. Presumably it is a form of *Rosa micrantha*, a species of wild rose described by Sir James E. Smith in

1813. *R. micrantha* is fairly frequent in England and is common in the south where it occurs on downs and heaths and sometimes in pastures. It is very like the Dog Rose in habit.

PLATE VIII

MUSK ROSE
ROSA MOSCHATA

The Musk Rose is doubtfully native in southern Europe. Its home appears to be the Himalayas, from Afghanistan to Nepal, where at from 3,000 feet to 8,000 feet it is the most characteristic rose. It was known to Theophrastus and was mentioned by Turner in his *A New Herball,* 1551 ; Gerard had three forms in his garden and there is a specimen of it in Plukenet's collections in the Sloane Herbarium at the British Museum. It was a favourite plant of Elizabethan gardens, and in Shakespeare it is exclusively allotted to Titania and her fairies. Hakluyt (1599) in his *Voyages* dates its introduction to this country: " The turkey cockes and hennes were brought about fifty yeres past, the Artichowe in time of King Henry the Eight, and of later times was procured out of Italy the Muske Rose plant, the Plumme called the Perdigwena, and two kindes more by the Lord Cromwell after his travel."

The Musk Rose is a vigorous climber with stout hooked thorns and rather thick blue-green narrow leaflets which are downy beneath. The flowers are ivory tinted and occur in large clusters in late summer ; the styles are united to form a solid column and the buds are long. The scent of the flowers is characteristic, and Bacon places the Musk Rose next to the violet " which above all others yields the sweetest smell in the air."

PLATE IX
CHINESE MONTHLY ROSE
ROSA CHINENSIS (R. *indica*)

This rose has many popular names, one of them being the Blush Monthly. It has been cultivated from time immemorial in the East, and it became one of the most popular roses grown in Europe. It appears to have been introduced to England by Sir Joseph Banks in 1789 and there is a specimen in the British Museum Herbarium of the original plants grown in Kew Garden. The first known specimen, however, also in the British Museum, is one dated 1704, from Gronovius, the Dutch Botanist. The only plants found in the wild were collected near Ichang in Central China and in the Nilgheri Hills, though it is generally regarded as not native in India.

The flowers are usually produced at the extremities of the branches in a kind of panicle and are slightly scented, though some varieties are very fragrant. Its hardiness, perpetual blooming and power of accommodation are remarkable.

The name Bengal Rose was formerly often applied to this rose because one variety reached Europe in a " Bengal ship." There is evidence that the double form was grown in China—where the history of gardening goes back to the earliest recorded times—in the tenth century.

PLATE X
CABBAGE ROSE, Provence Rose
ROSA CENTIFOLIA

This rose has been known in cultivation since the time of Herodotus. It is doubtful whether it is a true species or a modification of a single form through long cultivation. Its place of origin is unknown but is thought to be western Asia. It is the rose most referred to in poetry, prose and legend, and it has always been a great favourite with painters. Chaucer speaks of it : " Of Roses there were great wone So faire were never in Rone " (i.e., in Provence, at the mouth of the Rhone). Hamlet's " two Provincial Roses on my razed shoes," however, is a reference to rosettes and not to the flowers themselves.

The flowers of the Cabbage Rose are very fragrant. The sepals are never reflexed, the foliage is large with broad wrinkled leaflets, and fruit is rarely formed. Numerous varieties have arisen in cultivation. In Europe rose water is prepared chiefly from the Cabbage Rose, which was formerly grown at Mitcham for this purpose.

PLATE XI

POMPON ROSE, Rose de Meaux
ROSA POMPONIA

This is usually regarded as a diminutive form of the Cabbage Rose. The outer petals are pale pink and the colour and tone deepen up to the centre of the flower. English herbalists do not refer to it, but there are early references to it in France. The first mention of it in this country is in Aiton, *Hortus Kewensis*, 1789. Rose de Meaux is supposed to be named after Doménique Séguier, Bishop of Meaux in 1637, a lover of roses and a patron of horticulture. Diminutive forms occur sooner or later in all roses when grown from seed.

PLATE XII

DAMASK ROSE
ROSA DAMASCENA var. CELSIANA

The origin of the Damask Rose cannot now be traced. The frequent use of the name in Elizabethan times shows that some rose thought to have come from Damascus was well known, probably introduced into Europe by the Crusaders or some early travellers in the East. The gardens of Damascus have always impressed those visiting the city. Sir John Mandeville, in his *Voiage and Travaile*, says "In that Cytee of Damasce, there is gret plentee of Welles, and with in the Cytee and with oute, ben many fayre Gardynes and of dyverse frutes. Non other Cytee is not lyche in comparison to it, of fayre Gardynes, and of fayre desportes," and Kinglake in *Eothen* describes how that Damask Roses grow there to an immense height and size, and in profusion, "and load the slow air with their damask breath. There are no other flowers." If Hakluyt is correct we can date its introduction to this country within a short period for he writes in 1582, "In time of memory many things have been brought in that were not here before, as the Damaske Rose by Doctour Linaker, King Henry the Seventh and King Henrie the Eight's Physician"; Johnson says "The learned Linacre, who died in 1524, first introduced the Damask Rose from Italy."

The Damask Rose has a tall arching green stem, large hooked prickles and leathery leaves which are slightly pubescent underneath. The flowers have long deciduous sepals which reflex during flowering time; the fruit is elongated and turns bright red and pulpy in September.

Redouté figures seven varieties of the Damask Rose. The most attractive of these is var. *Celsiana* which is seen in many of Van Huysum's finest paintings; in the gardens of Haarlem it was known by his name and was introduced to France by Cels.

The Damask Rose grows on Omar Khayyám's grave at Nashipier. Seeds from it were germinated at Kew and thence a shoot planted on the tomb of Edward Fitzgerald.

The Damask Rose is grown in Bulgaria and in India for distilling Attar (Otto) of Roses.

PLATE XIII

SULPHUR ROSE

ROSA HEMISPHAERICA (R. *sulfurea*)

The introduction of this rose to England is related by Parkinson who calls it the double Yellow Rose; " which first was procured to be brought into England, by Master Nicholas Lete, a worthy Merchant of London, and a great lover of flowers, from Constantinople, which (as wee heare) was first brought thither from Syria ; but perished quickly both with him, and with all other to whom hee imparted it : yet afterwards it was sent to Master John de Franqueville, a Merchant also of London, and a great lover of all rare plants, as well as flowers, from which is sprung the greatest store, that is now flourishing in this Kingdome." Its introduction to western Europe had been brought about a few years previously in a remarkable manner. Clusius, the eminent Netherlands botanist, while on a visit to Vienna saw a paper model of a garden which had been brought from Constantinople, with a double yellow rose among the flowers. By the aid of one of his numerous correspondents he succeeded in obtaining one of the roses from there. It is probably a native of western Asia. It is now exceedingly rare in this country.

PLATE XIV

MOSS ROSE

ROSA CENTIFOLIA var. MUSCOSA
(R. *muscosa*)

The Moss Rose was not known until the beginning of the eighteenth century. It was first mentioned in a sale catalogue of plants by R. Furber of Kensington, 1724, and figured in his *Twelve Months of Flowers*, 1730. Philip

Miller, the famous curator of the Chelsea Physic Garden, described it in 1760 in the *Illustrations* to his classic *Gardeners' Dictionary*, and there he says " This Rose has not been many Years known in England: The first time I saw it was in the Year 1727, in the Garden of Dr. Boerhaave near Leyden, who was so good as to give me One of the Plants; but from whence it originally came I could not learn." There is a specimen from Chelsea in the British Museum Herbarium dated 1735. The Moss Rose was mentioned in the 1720 edition of the catalogue of the Leyden garden and as it did not appear in the first edition, 1710, we may assume that it arose as a sport between these dates.

The White Moss Rose appeared as a bud variation of the old Moss Rose in 1735, and the Striped Moss Rose as a sport of the White Moss Rose in 1790. Varieties of Moss Ross became numerous and by the middle of last century numbered more than fifty.

The evidence for the Moss Rose having been known at Carcassonne as early as 1696 is unreliable. As this country played so large a part in the development of the Moss Rose it was often stated that it originated here. Alluding to this Thory remarks that when the origin of a plant is unknown, the English immediately claim it as indigenous to their own country.

PLATE XV

ROSA PROVINCIALIS var. BULLATA
(R. *centifolia* var. *bullata*)

This rose was formerly found in most gardens. It is said to have been a novelty imported from Holland in 1815. It has beautiful fragrant flowers and curiously large and voluminous leaflets which turn a fine bronze tint in summer.

It is probably not a variety of the Cabbage Rose but of the Provins Rose, which is one of the earliest known roses, mentioned by classical writers and given in Gerard's Catalogue. The popular name of the latter is supposed to have arisen from the fact that the Rose was brought from Syria by Thibaut le Chansonnier, who cultivated it in his garden at Provins. For a long time the cultivation of these roses was a considerable source of income to the district.

PLATE XVI

ROSA GALLICA var. REGALIS

This is a very charming variety of the French Rose. *See* Plate VI.

REFERENCES

A. M. T. Amherst—*A History of Gardening in England*, 3rd ed., 1910.

E. A. Bunyard—*Old Garden Roses*, 1935.

H. N. E. Ellacombe—*The Plant-lore & Garden-Craft of Shakespeare*, 1st ed., 1878, 2nd ed. 1884.

W. Paul—*The Rose Garden*, 9th ed., 1888.

E. S. Rohde—*The Old English Herbals*, 1922.

E. Willmott—*The Genus Rosa*, 1910-1914.

The Rose Annual of the National Rose Society, 1907 *et seq.*

PLATES

I ROSA NITIDA

II YELLOW AUSTRIAN BRIAR

III APPLE ROSE

IV COPPER AUSTRIAN BRIAR

V   DOG ROSE

VI ROSA MUNDI

VII ROSA MICRANTHA

VIII MUSK ROSE

IX   CHINESE MONTHLY ROSE

X CABBAGE ROSE, PROVENCE ROSE

XI POMPON ROSE

XII DAMASK ROSE

XIII SULPHUR ROSE

XIV MOSS ROSE

XV ROSA PROVINCIALIS

XVI ROSA GALLICA